CW00536912

A PRIEST'S GUIDE

TO

HEARING CONFESSIONS

A PRIEST'S GUIDE

TO

HEARING CONFESSIONS

By Fr Michael Woodgate

CATHOLIC TRUTH SOCIETY
PUBLISHERS TO THE HOLY SEE

A Priest's Guide to Hearing Confessions: Published 2008 by the Incorporated Catholic Truth Society, 40-46 Harleyford Road, London, SE11 5AY Tel: 020 7640 0042   Fax: 020 7640 0046. Copyright © 2008 The Incorporated Catholic Truth Society.

website: www.cts-online.org.uk

ISBN 978 1 86082 530 9

CONTENTS

Documents referred to in the text

Catechism of the Catholic Church, 1994
Misericordia Dei, Apostolic Letter of Pope John Paul II
The Code of Canon Law, 1983
The Cumberledge Report, 2007
The Nolan Report, 2001
The Rite of Penance, 1976
Sacramentorum Sanctitatis Tutela, 2001, Pope John Paul II
Safe and Sound,
Vademecum for Confessors concerning some aspects of the morality of conjugal life, 1997, Pontifical Council for the Family

INTRODUCTION

Older priests will remember the various manuals for confessors and manuals of moral theology. Many being ordained to-day will have little knowledge of their existence. This is not to say that their formation will have been lacking in confessional teaching and practice, but it is felt that a short guide to the practice of celebrating the Sacrament of Reconciliation might be helpful. This small book makes no attempt to be an equivalent modern manual and the author is well aware of its deficiencies, but is grateful to those priests who have been helpful in their advice and constructive criticism. With the increasing complexity of society and, sad to say, poor catechesis in some quarters, the confessor can be faced with more difficult situations than his forebears and by the very nature of the seal of the Sacrament, it is not easy for him to discuss those situations with fellow-priests, especially in his own deanery or even diocese. We hope this modest publication may prove helpful to priests of longer experience, as well as to those more recently ordained.

INTRODUCTION

CHAPTER I

BACKGROUND TO THE SACRAMENT

Background to the Sacrament

The Church's rules about and attitudes towards certain sins have changed over the years. You might even say that the relationship between priest and penitent has evolved in such a way that a penitent today is more likely to have a warmer welcome than one confessing (say) fifty years ago. That is not to say that there have not always been priests of great tenderness and compassion, it is simply to say that such approaches to the penitent are more frequent than they were.

Throughout the centuries there have been changes in penitential discipline and in the practice of celebrating the Sacrament. For example, in the 2nd century it was thought that there were three sins which the Church could not remit and those who committed them were excluded from Holy Communion for life. They were: acts of idolatry, acts of sexual immorality and murder. In the 3rd century, discipline was modified with regard to those three irremissible sins. Pope Callistus, for example, re-admitted post-baptismal adulterers. Cyprian re-admitted those involved in idolatrous acts and with regard to murder, the Council of Ancyra at the beginning of the 4th century admitted murderers to be reconciled with the Church on their deathbed. The procedure for absolution for such serious sins involved being enrolled in the order of penitents and then penance would ensue. A special dress was worn and a special seat was allotted in church. Penitents were dismissed at Mass just before the Prayers of the Faithful. The process normally ended with absolution of penitents at the Mass of Reconciliation of Penitents on Maundy Thursday, due penance having been performed during Lent. But the story did not necessarily end there. Only one penance was permitted after baptism for a serious sin. Why? Perhaps because it proved to be a compromise between rigorists and liberals. Familiar story?

The system just outlined worked reasonably well in the Ante-Nicean era when Christians, by and large, took their faith seriously. But from the 4th century onwards it started to break down. As the Church began to change its composition, so its discipline changed, too. Large numbers were baptized in infancy and when Christianity became 'fashionable' in the Roman Empire, the Church grew rapidly in numbers. There was a growing practice of delaying penance until the deathbed and many Christians who fell into open sin simply accepted exclusion from Holy Communion, and those who fell into secret sin might receive the Blessed Sacrament with a bad conscience or simply wait until they were dying. There was a dropping off in general of lay people receiving Holy Communion from the 4th century onwards.

The system was modified in the 7th century through the influence of Irish monasticism, which spread into France and Italy and may originally have been disseminated by English missionary monks in the Netherlands and Germany. This modification combined some of the austerities of the old system of penance with the growing practice of deathbed penance. Another change was that penance could be administered by the priest and not only by the bishop. Also, there was no public admittance to the order of penitents. But the penance imposed was comparable to that under the old system, e.g. weeks of fasting. The penitent might go to the local monastery to do that penance. The season most commonly used was that of Lent and so Lent gains in importance at this time. Shrove Tuesday became the popular day for setting the penance and Easter for absolution, given privately by the priest. This took the public humiliation out of penance. Also, it was possible to do penance again if the same sin was committed. Absolution could also be given for less serious sins, which was known as a 'confession of devotion.' Devout Christians were resorting to holy men for counsel even though their sin was light. Penance and absolution were combined with the counsel. The Fourth Lateran Council of 1215 included as one of the Paschal Precepts the obligation of confessing once a year, whether in grave sin or not. The present situation in England and Wales is that every Catholic who has reached the age of discretion must, if in mortal sin, celebrate the Sacrament at least once a year. (Canon 989 & Catechism § 1457). Broadly speaking, the practice of the Sacrament of Penance changed very little until the Second Vatican Council.

Users of this booklet will be familiar with the *Rite of Penance* which was approved for use in the dioceses of England, Wales and Scotland in 1976 following a decree of the Council and published by the authority of Pope Paul VI. Although reference will be made to it in this manual and sections of it quoted, we make no attempt to reproduce its contents as it is expected that every priest will possess his own copy.

CHAPTER II

THE PRIEST IN THE CONFESSIONAL

THE PRIEST IN THE CONFESSIONAL

For every valid sacrament four things are necessary: Matter, Minister, Rite and Intention.

Let us take each one in turn as it concerns the Sacrament of Reconciliation:

1. Matter

There are two parts:

(a) The *remote* matter is sin. It is remote because it must happen *before* the sacrament is celebrated.

(b) The *immediate* matter is the three acts of the penitent: Confession, Contrition and Satisfaction.

Both must be present before absolution can be given.

All sin is matter for absolution, but there is **necessary** or **grave** matter which needs sacramental absolution and **light** or **free** matter which needs only acts of contrition for forgiveness. Of course, all sin is displeasing, indeed hateful to God, but for practical reasons we make this distinction. We need when teaching about the sacrament to distinguish between sin which is a bar to Holy Communion and sin which is venial and therefore is not.

The constituent elements of serious (mortal) sin are:

(a) Grave matter.

(b) Full knowledge. A sin is only formally computable to someone if they commit it with full knowledge. It remains, however, materially wrong.

(c) Full or deliberate consent. If, e.g., someone is half asleep, drugged or drunk, then he/she is not sinning with full consent.

Where the matter is absent

There may be occasions in the confessional when not even venial or light matter is confessed, when, e.g. a penitent has prepared insufficiently. In this case, the priest may properly ask permission to examine his/her conscience for them, perhaps by going through, e.g., the Ten Commandments, the Beatitudes, the Fruits of the Spirit (*Galatians* 5:22) or the Seven Capital Sins. It is far better to do this than to send a penitent away and tell them (however politely) to make a proper preparation. It takes courage to come to the confessional and having arrived one doesn't want anyone to go away empty-handed.

Sometimes, a person with learning difficulties may come to confession but have nothing to say or not know where to begin. It goes without saying that the priest will be extra gentle, and judge whether it would be helpful to ask them some questions to produce matter for absolution, or whether it would be best to say a prayer and give them a blessing. Clearly, this is an area where enormous sensitivity is needed. Some penitents may have a severe speech impediment, but be perfectly capable of recalling matter for absolution. Indeed, they may be extremely intelligent people, but the priest will have great difficulty in hearing what they say. The same may be true of those whose first language is not English. It goes without saying that the confessor needs to listen very carefully and may need to ask them to repeat something they have said. Again, great sensitivity is needed, not to speak of patience.

Occasionally, someone will come to confession who really has no sins to confess because of the holiness of their lives. What they confess is likely to be an imperfection or two, or sometimes they will simply say that they cannot remember any sins, but "I'm sure there must be some, Father". Again, the confessor should not send them away even with only a blessing. The priest may then say something like: "Do you mind if I ask you some questions?" and go through (say) the

Ten Commandments which may jog their memory, though this needs to be done intelligently and helpfully (a bare: "Have you committed murder?" might illicit a funny answer!). If this proves unproductive, the penitent can be invited to make a renewed act of penitence for some past serious sin which has already been absolved and then absolution can be given.

Without in any way wishing to undermine the integrity of the sacrament, in cases of real doubt it is better to give absolution than to withhold it.

The unconscious dying

If such a person had asked to see the priest before becoming unconscious, then he may be given absolution without confession. It can be assumed that he or she has sinned and wanted to see the priest for the very purpose of receiving forgiveness.

Major incidents

Here there is usually no time to deal with individuals, so the priest should give a general absolution – one of the few instances where this is not only permitted but necessary. (See also section below: *When absolution should be withheld p. 115*.)

Contrition

The mere fact that a person has come to confession makes a *prima facie* case for contrition. The four marks of contrition required in the confessional are:

(a) Internal - real sorrow of the will - the only part of us under our own control - not just of the emotions.

(b) Supernatural - arising from a supernatural motive, preferably love of God, not merely fear of human punishment or public disgrace (Cf. II *Corinthians* 7:10).

(c) Supreme - that is, it must be the dominating factor in our life. What will happen tomorrow is of no concern.

(d) Universal - contrition must cover all grave sins committed.

If a confessor is concerned about a person's contrition, he can make two tests:

(a) Ask if he/she really does resolve not to sin again (not simply be hot under the collar about it!), and

(b) ask if he/she is willing to avoid the occasions of sin. There can be a danger of carelessness if someone has come to confession under some pressure (a child perhaps, persuaded by parents). The other danger is from those who come out of habit. If you are concerned about the seeming lack of penitence, say something to the penitent about our Lord's sacrifice, about what it cost him to redeem us.

Confession

All grave sins must be confessed and the confessor would normally assume that this has been done and would only intervene if he had some first-hand knowledge of some grave sin. Grave sin must be confessed clearly. If it is not, then the confessor must question prudently and must never absolve without knowing what he is questioning. Ask questions only within the limits required for absolution and within the limits required for counselling.

Satisfaction

A penance must be set either as a real satisfaction to God, or as a token satisfaction. Also satisfaction may need to be made to others if grave injury has been done, especially in matters of theft or slander.

Absolution

The outward and effective sign of this sacrament is the words of absolution, which a priest should know by heart. It has to be said that this is not an easy formula to memorize and those ordained later in life probably find it harder than younger men. Some priests keep a copy in their wallet or notebook, so that it is always with them and the newly-ordained of any age would surely find this a valuable practice. However, it is worth remembering that the *essential words* of the formula are the *"Ego te absolvo" – "I absolve you from your sins in the name of the Father, and of the Son, and of the Holy Spirit. Amen."* (N.B. In immediate danger of death, these are the only words necessary.) As the priest pronounces the words he extends his right hand (or both hands) over the head of the penitent and as he says the final words (quoted above) he makes the sign of the cross over the penitent.

Dismissal of penitent

The *Rite of Penance* (Chapter 1, § 49) sets out a number of formulae for blessing and dismissing the individual penitent, with an emphasis on praise and growth in the Christian life.

2. Minister of penance

The power to absolve sacramentally is given to a priest at his ordination, but he must also have the *authority* to exercise that power, i.e. the requisite faculties and the jurisdiction over whom he can exercise those faculties. (N.B. Jurisdiction may be either ordinary or delegated. The first is acquired by reason of a benefice or office and the second granted by the direct commission or concession of an ecclesiastical superior). The diocesan priest will receive those faculties in writing by virtue of his office, or by virtue of a concession by the Ordinary of either the place of incardination, or where he has a domicile and he can exercise it everywhere, unless in a particular place the local Ordinary has refused it. (For full details see Canons § 965-986.) Any priest, even though he lacks the faculty to hear confessions, can do so, validly and lawfully, in danger of death. He can also absolve from excommunication in the same circumstances. This, of course, includes a priest who is inhibited from exercising his priesthood, even one who is excommunicate. A priest may also absolve a partner in sin when in danger of death.

(*See also Censures, p. 129.*)

The sacramental seal is inviolable and if (as in rare circumstances) an interpreter has to be present, he or she must observe the same secrecy, or indeed anyone who has obtained knowledge of a sin through the Sacrament. Certain sins are "reserved", which means they are removed from the jurisdiction of, e.g., the parish priest or his assistant. (*See also Censures, p. 129.*)

Canon § 970 says that a faculty may only be given to a priest whose suitability has been established either by examination or by some other means. But a penitent might also expect from a priest (even though it does not affect absolution) a man who is growing in virtue. Some personal qualifications might be: goodness, knowledge and prudence. Let us say a few words about these.

Goodness

This is about holiness of life which includes both moral and spiritual holiness. A confessor who is not leading a moral life himself will have difficulty in judging and in helping others to lead a moral life. A confessor who is leading a moral life but not a spiritual one, will have difficulty in helping others to lead a spiritual life.

Knowledge

A confessor needs knowledge of moral principles. It was St Teresa of Avila who inveighed against those who lacked knowledge of those principles.

Prudence

This is the ability to apply moral and spiritual principles to particular cases. The confessor needs knowledge of life and human nature and how to apply to these the knowledge gained from study, books and lectures.

Hearing confessions involves being a spiritual judge (which is primary) and being a physician (which is secondary) and so:

(a) As a *judge* he will have to decide whether there is any sin to absolve, whether it has been confessed accurately, whether there is sufficient sorrow, whether the sin is light or grave.

(b) As a *physician* he must provide particular remedies for particular sins, e.g. certain occasions which have led to sin may have to be given up – this is the way of *precept*. At other times he may have to go more generally by way of *counsel*, e.g. urging the penitent to improve his whole moral and spiritual life – urging conversion of life.

The confessor must also take into account his own temperament when doing either of these things, e.g. he may be temperamentally harsh in judging others and therefore must be more charitable or reasonable. Or he may be temperamentally easygoing and so must cultivate a deeper sense of the majesty, of the glory of God which is outraged by sin.

Remote preparation for hearing confessions

How does the confessor acquire these three qualifications of goodness, knowledge and prudence?

(a) By prayer - not just a few minutes before going into the confessional, but by the daily practice of the spiritual life.

(b) By reading - especially works of moral and ascetical theology. But novels (e.g. famously, Graham Greene's) which give a deep insight into human nature are also worth reading, as are biographies. The lives of saintly men and women can help to inspire, guide, instruct and enthuse, and can sometimes provide good models, but one needs to be both sensible and sensitive about this. The saints are not always to be imitated!

(c) By conversations with experienced confessors. But, as we indicated earlier, this is not as straightforward as it sounds, because of the seal. Diocesan ongoing formation programmes sometimes include sessions which can be helpful in this respect.

(d) By actually hearing confessions. Remember the difference between a confessional and a pulpit: a confessional is primarily a place where the *penitent* speaks, the pulpit is the place where the *preacher* speaks. We need to remember also that there will always be the penitent who comes into the confessional primarily to ask for help and not primarily to confess. He or she comes because they know that this is where they can guarantee finding a priest without the uncertainty of what will happen if they ring the presbytery bell. Such people should not be sent away with a flea in their ear, of course, but may be encouraged to wait until the last penitent has left, or make an appointment for what they really *need*, e.g. pastoral counselling or spiritual direction.

Inevitably, a confessor, especially one new to the priesthood, will make mistakes or will consider, by hindsight, that he could have handled it differently. But we must not forget that the "Third Party" - the Holy Spirit – is always present and that the penitent has gone away with what he has primarily come for, and that is absolution, which only a priest can give.

3. The Rite of the Sacrament
The three rites are clearly set out in the *Rite of Penance*, Chapters I, II, and III.

4. The Intention of the Sacrament
The effects of the sacrament of penance are to reconcile us with God and with the Church after grave sin. "The whole power of the Sacrament of Penance consists in restoring us to God's grace, and joining us with him in an intimate friendship" (*Catechism of the Catholic Church*, § 1468). The *Catechism of the Catholic Church* goes on to say that the Sacrament "has also a revitalizing effect on the life of the Church which suffered from the sin of one of her members." Every celebration of the sacrament is for the penitent a further step on the road to conversion of life.

CHAPTER III

THE SEAL OF CONFESSION

The Seal of Confession

The seal imposed upon the confessor is the obligation not to reveal anything heard during the confession or deduced from it. It binds absolutely and admits of no exception whatsoever. The *Code of Canon Law* is quite clear and because it is so important, we include it here (Canons § 983-984).

Can. 983

§ 1. The sacramental seal is inviolable. Accordingly, it is absolutely forbidden for a confessor in any way to betray the penitent, for any reason whatsoever, whether by word or in any other fashion.

§ 2. An interpreter, if there is one, is also obliged to observe this secret, as are all others who in any way whatever have come to a knowledge of sins from a confession.

Can. 984

§ 1. The confessor is wholly forbidden to use knowledge acquired in confession to the detriment of the penitent, even when all danger of disclosure is excluded.

§ 2. A person who is in authority may not in any way, for the purpose of external governance, use knowledge about sins which has at any time come to him from the hearing of a confession.

The penalty for a confessor who violates the seal is a *latae sententiae* excommunication reserved to the Congregation for the Doctrine of the Faith (CDF) (cf Canon 1388 § 1). Also, an interpreter and others who have come to know the sins of another through confession and who violate the seal incur a just penalty, not excluding excommunication. Since a decree promulgated by the CDF in 1988, and approved by the Holy Father, a penalty (excommunication) has been established for those who divulge the contents of a sacramental confession by means of social communications or who record it in any way on some device. (*vid.* AAS 80 (1988) 1367).

When teaching about the sacrament of reconciliation, it is good practice to ask one's catechumens to observe the seal also, even though they are not canonically obliged. The chief, though not only, reason for this is that it protects the priest from what could later be a false accusation. If the seal were not absolute, who would ever risk going to confession?

A breach of the seal can occur directly or indirectly.

Direct breach

This *can* happen as a result of sheer malice, though it would be rare on the part of a confessor. One may come across a parishioner talking about the seal having been broken, in which case it would be strongly advisable to get from them a written statement to that effect. If they are merely slandering then action must be taken against them.

If a confessor does break the seal, it is more likely to be out of carelessness. It is essential to keep the two spheres of knowledge about one's penitents quite separate from the very beginning. A priest must avoid having a reputation as a gossip, however light-hearted that gossip may be.

Indirect breach

This is much more likely than a direct breach and some examples would be:

(a) Using too loud a voice in the confessional – either confessor or penitent.

(b) Speaking about sins confessed so as to make the identity of the penitent recognizable.

(c) To say of a penitent that he/she has *not* confessed a particular sin implying, for example, an incomplete confession.

(d) Speaking of sins known outside the confessional, but adding details known only from inside it.

(e) Warning parents to take particular precautions after their offspring have confessed a particular sin. (E.g. It might be tempting to help protect a young penitent from the occasion of sin by warning the parents not to leave money around.)

(f) Two confessors discussing a particular person when both have heard that person's confession at different times.

(g) Preaching against particular sins which the confessor knows only through the confessional. This is one which demands great sensitivity as the Mass lections may be ideal for preaching about such sins. On the other hand, sins do need to be addressed in homilies!

(h) Speaking to a penitent outside the confessional of sins known only from inside it. Even if one is alone with a penitent (outside the confessional), the confessor must ask permission to break the seal. On the other hand, if the penitent him or herself starts talking of what he/she confessed inside the confessional, then that is tacit permission to do so.

(i) Changing one's attitude towards a penitent because of sins heard in the confessional.

Further useful points to bear in mind

A confessor may admit to a third party that he has heard someone's confession, but can say no more. Even this fact should only be admitted when absolutely necessary. Such a person needs to be a "proper person", i.e. have some some pastoral connection with the penitent. The confessor may never say more than: *"Audivi"* (*"I have heard"*) with regard to either sin, penance, advice or whether absolution was given or not. If asked by an "improper person", then he may say: "Why don't you ask so-and-so yourself?" If they persist, he will need to tell them to mind their own business!

The seal is not broken if a confessor speaks in the confessional of sins confessed on a previous occasion, but he should not do so without good reason.

A confessor may speak to a penitent about matter heard in the confessional immediately after the confession on the grounds that it forms one moral whole with it. For example, a person may have asked for advice which will take quite a time and one does not wish to keep others waiting. So penance and absolution can be given and then the penitent may come afterwards to talk to the priest either in the confessional (especially if it is a reconciliation room providing a chair) or in the presbytery.

If one is hearing confessions during a retreat and the counsel is separated from the confession by a day or so, then both can be treated as a whole. A similar case might arise if someone is dying and one drops in each day. Such a person might ask if they remembered to confess a particular sin when they confessed perhaps a day or two ago. You may in such circumstances say "Yes" or "No", without asking their permission to break the seal. The dying must be troubled as little as possible.

The seal also binds a third party who gets knowledge of matter revealed in the confessional, e.g. someone in church who accidentally (or even deliberately) overhears what is said, or reads the confession of another when it serves as the actual confession, or as a means of actually confessing, or has been left in the confessional or been lost by the confessor, but not if the penitent has lost it or is in possession of it outside the confessional, but if there is a doubt whether the penitent or the confessor left the script in the confessional, it must be considered as under the seal. Another example, of course, would be an interpreter who is clearly bound by the seal.

A confessor may occasionally wish to consult a more experienced confessor, but it is important to ensure that the second opinion does not identify the penitent. If so, then he is bound by the seal.

Penitents may give permission to a confessor to speak to someone about their sins outside the confessional and to consult a third party to obtain advice, but this must be done discreetly. The permission must be given directly and not assumed and if the penitent withdraws the permission, this withdrawal must be accepted.

Remember, that although penitents are not bound by the seal, they are bound by the obligation of a natural and committed secret concerning the things spoken of by the confessor in confession if revealing them would harm the confessor or bring contempt to the Sacrament in any way.

CHAPTER IV

ADVERTISING THE SACRAMENT

ADVERTISING THE SACRAMENT

There should, of course, be regular Confession times advertised in every parish (and in every church or Mass centre of that parish), both on a notice board and in the weekly newsletter. Likewise, seasonal services of reconciliation should also be advertised well in advance, as these give penitents the opportunity of going to a confessor other than their parish priest and they will not need to make a special journey elsewhere, often difficult just before Christmas and Easter. It is also good to make advertised times inclusive, e.g. 11 am – 12 noon, rather than give only the starting time.

Time in the confessional never need be wasted – spiritual reading, the rosary, the Divine Office, other prayer can all be usefully offered during the waiting times. Times must be arranged to suit the needs of as many people as possible, which is why morning and afternoon/evening on Saturday should normally feature, as well as a time or two during the week. Much will depend upon the local situation. Town centre churches may well be used by shoppers and working people from other parishes, so a lunchtime slot could be very useful. Although people should learn to respect advertised times and not call at the presbytery for a priest just because it suits them, a priest should be prepared to hear a confession without fuss or hesitation if he is available. One needs to remember that there are those who genuinely cannot manage any of the advertised times because of their working hours or other genuine commitments. In not a few parishes there will be someone who wants to make his or her confession just before Mass. Sometimes it is necessary to say: "Make your Communion and I will hear your confession as soon as possible after Mass. You are obviously penitent and desire absolution." In these days, when most parishes do not have assistant priests (unless fortunate enough to have a retired one), it is not always easy to cover all advertised confession times.

However, this must be seen as an absolute priority, so make sure that the times advertised can always be kept except, of course, in the case of a dire emergency. You may, for example, find it best not to advertise times on the permanent notice-board, but to say something like this: "Confessions – see weekly notices in glass frame" and to make sure that your notice paper in the glass frame is outside the church and not only inside, unless there is 24 hour access to it. Some people are reluctant (for whatever reason) to ring up the presbytery. Incidentally, if you have a recorded message on your answerphone giving Mass times, make sure you also include confession times.

Never say: "Confessions on request" or even worse, "By appointment." This can be very off-putting; and what does it mean in practice? In the first instance, it makes it sound as though the Sacrament of Reconciliation is not a frequent or common ministry, readily available. Secondly, it is another of those discouraging notices which can deter the nervous penitent, or one coming back to the Sacrament after a long absence. Even to advertise "Confessions after Mass" can be a little unhelpful because indeterminate. After every Mass? After the priest has spoken to everyone leaving? After he has had a cup of coffee? It is much better to give an actual starting time and deliberately make a point of going into the confessional – perhaps ten minutes after Mass. It would be best to exclude Sundays, as there is usually a host of people who quite legitimately need to speak to the clergy after

Sunday Masses and in any case a priest should be prepared to spend time with his people then, unless he has another Mass immediately following.

In addition to advertising times, a parish priest should ensure that the sacrament is mentioned from time to time in the notices and especially, of course, before Christmas and Easter. It is always best to emphasize the joy of celebrating the sacrament, as well as the obligation.

In his Apostolic Letter *Misericordia Dei*, Pope John Paul II requested that confessions be especially available before Masses, and even during Mass if other priests are available, in order to meet the needs of the faithful.

Every now and then the homily should highlight the sacrament and even remind a congregation how to prepare for and celebrate it. Fear of returning after a long absence is often due to having forgotten what to do. Assure those who may have had bad experiences in the past, that this will now be most unlikely.

CHAPTER V

PLACE FOR THE CELEBRATION OF THE SACRAMENT

PLACE FOR THE CELEBRATION
OF THE SACRAMENT

It is clearly laid down in Canon Law (§ 964) that the proper place for hearing confessions is a church or oratory and norms are issued by the Episcopal Conferences, but with this proviso: *"...confessionals, which the faithful who so wish may freely use, are located in an open place, and fitted with a fixed grille between the penitent and the confessor."* Some older churches have retained the traditional confessional "box". Others have added – and most churches built since Vatican II have included – a "reconciliation room" where the penitent has the opportunity of making his or her confession either face-to-face with the priest or behind a grille. It is important to ensure that the penitent can exercise his or her right to make their confession behind a grille; it is also the right of the priest to be able to hear confessions in this way. There have been instances of priests strongly dissuading penitents from this practice. There may be occasions when it is appropriate to hear a confession outside the church, e.g., when someone comes to the presbytery for spiritual direction or a for a pastoral interview which results in their wishing to make their confession and seek absolution. Likewise, of course, a confession may be heard during a sick call either at home or in hospital. On all these occasions it is essential to ensure that secrecy is maintained.

We have probably all heard "horror stories" about the confessions of the deaf. The problem is usually not the penitent him or herself, but the confessor needing to raise his voice in order to be heard. The priest must ensure he is very aware that his voice could be heard outside the confessional and moderate it accordingly, but whatever happens, it is essential that the penitent is clear about the penance that is given.

Every parish should have built into its code of practice regarding children and vulnerable adults, arrangements for hearing their confessions. A priest should familiarize himself with this code.

CHAPTER VI

THE PROCESS OF HEARING A CONFESSION

THE PROCESS OF HEARING A CONFESSION

The confessor should normally seek the guidance of the Holy Spirit before he enters the confessional. Having donned a purple stole (and maybe vested also in cassock and cotta or alb), he goes to his seat and awaits the arrival of the first penitent. Some confessionals have a system of coloured lights, e.g. green when free, red when occupied. It is most important to familiarize oneself with the system and to remember to use it each time. If the confession is to be face-to-face, one can often get an impression of whether the penitent is particularly nervous, in tears, or any state that needs special sensitivity. But often the tone of voice is enough to convey something of the state of mind. Despite the way in which the present rite is structured, most penitents will still begin with the words: "Bless me Father, for I have sinned. My last confession was 'x' weeks/months ago." The confessor will then make the sign of the cross over the penitent, thus responding to the call for a blessing and if he wishes to follow the rite in detail, he will use (from the *Rite of Penance*) one of the forms for the *Invitation to Trust*.

The rite then states that a penitent unknown to the confessor should indicate his or her state of life and "anything else which may help the confessor in exercising his ministry". In practice this is not commonly done, except by priests or religious. The confessor may then read a passage of Scripture (or the penitent may be invited to do this) and then will allow the penitent to confess his/her sins without interruption, which he/she may do using a recognized formula (e.g. "I confess to almighty God..."). As the rite (§ 46) states: *"If necessary the priest helps the penitent to make an integral confession and gives him suitable counsel. The priest should make sure he adapts his counsel to the penitent's circumstances."* Whilst hearing the confession the confessor needs not only to *listen very carefully*, but to make a mental note of any serious sin and any sins that he feels need particular focus when giving counsel. Sometimes a question or two will be required for elucidation or information.

As the penitent confesses, the confessor must be patient with anyone who is finding it difficult and not interrupt, unless it becomes absolutely necessary and then only to help, not to try and hasten. As the confession proceeds, the confessor must, as we have just said, make a mental note of anything which needs to be dealt with afterwards, i.e. anything incompletely confessed, anything that requires restoration by the penitent and anything that simply needs counsel. It is best to forget anything else, especially matter which is clearly not sinful (though he may wish to tell the penitent so). No penitent should be interrupted, (except in the extreme circumstance noted above), as this can disturb his or her flow and even cause him or her to leave out a sin or sins. The priest must be very sensitive to the penitent's feelings. A long pause in the middle of a confession must be accepted. It could be, for example, that the penitent is summoning up his/her courage to tell their worst sin (worst, or most embarrassing, in their estimation, anyway). If the confessor says: "Is that all?" the Evil One may quickly put it into the heart of the penitent to say: "Yes, Father" and so that sin is left unconfessed and the penitent will go away a very unhappy person.

Asking questions

Never ask unnecessary questions, but when a question is required you need to distinguish between acting only as a confessor and acting as a spiritual director to that penitent as well. Normally, it is only in the case of grave sin that a confessor acting *only* as confessor need ask questions. For example, in the case of a grave sin (or in order to establish whether it is a grave sin), the priest needs to know the circumstances, *viz.* whether the sin was in thought only, or in word and deed as well; whether the sinful act was complete or partial; whether it was deliberate or inculpable ignorance; whether it was with full consent of the will; whether it was committed alone or with others, with persons in one's care; whether the sin was committed in order to cause grave scandal; whether it was committed only once or more than once, frequently or habitually. These kind of questions are not only helpful, but also necessary if one is to give relevant counsel. Of course, the questioning must always be confined to the matter that has been confessed. Questioning may be needed to help ascertain more clearly what the penitent is saying. Once again, it must be emphasized that one may not question on any sin not confessed even if the confessor is morally certain that the penitent has committed a certain sin: e.g. the confessor may have heard from another that the penitent on an occasion used foul or abusive language, but he/she does not confess it. If the confessor heard it himself, then he *may* mention it, but it must be a *grave* sin or at least the matter must be grave. If a penitent has told you something outside the confessional but does not mention it inside, then the priest must use his discretion.

There is also the example of an unmarried couple coming to confession at the same time. One confesses (let us say) to sexual intercourse, but the other does not. However tempting it may be to ask about this, one may *not*. In any case, the act could have been committed with a third party. If one does strongly suspect that the penitent is holding back a grave sin, then it would be in order, once he or she has finished their confession, to ask the colourless question: "Is there anything else?" Since it is the priest's duty to help people confess all their grave sins and try not to allow them to make a sacrilegious confession, there could be a real pastoral tension here, but the integrity of the penitent's confession must be paramount. Of course, one of the problems faced by priests these days is that not all one's penitents are aware of what is a grave sin. Much catechesis is required - and should not be shirked –

by the priest in his homilies. In any case, questions should be put in a kindly way and never be construed as cross-examination.

When it *is* necessary to ask questions for clarification about a particular sin, they should be asked from the greater to the lesser. For example, if a penitent says: "I have stolen", the confessor may want to say something like this: "You say you have stolen. Do you mean you've robbed the bank, or, you've been breaking and entering?" The penitent may then reply: "Oh no, Father, I took some copying paper from work because I was a bit short at home and wanted to type some letters that evening". In such a case, the paper could be restored. But in the case of the sixth commandment, the questioning should proceed in reverse order. For example, the penitent might confess: "I have been impure" and the priest may then say: "Do you mean you've entertained some impure thoughts?" The penitent could then answer: "Well no, Father, it was rather worse than that. I'm afraid I committed self-abuse" or even "I slept with my boy/girl friend". Now if the priest had said: "You mean you've committed adultery/fornication?" the penitent could feel very hurt, being one who has always led a very chaste life and knows the priest wasn't making a joke of it in order to lighten the situation. Likewise, the penitent might say, "Oh, nothing as bad as that, Father. I just allowed my feelings to run away with me", thus trying to avoid confessing to self-abuse, and perhaps silencing the priest, who thought he had got the whole picture. There really is a difference when it comes to sexual sin, however much today's society (and even, dare one say, some Catholics) might treat it as though it were no different than, say, greed. Now, clearly, we don't want to make sins against the sixth commandment any more difficult to confess than they usually are for most penitents, but nor do we want to encourage them to wrap them up or give mixed messages. On the other hand, we don't want to emphasize the culpability of sexual sin so that it seems out of all proportion.

Counsel

The confessor must keep a balance, but if he is to give sound and helpful counsel he must have a clear picture of the sin. If, for example, a penitent confesses to looking at pornographic sites on the internet (a not uncommon sin these days), he needs to help him/her to take strong measures to deal with this, short perhaps, of throwing one's computer into the nearest river. It may also be worth adding that the viewing of certain sites and certainly downloading them is a criminal offence. Penitents who have become addicts may well be urged to get some counselling or therapy. This goes, of course, for other addictions which may or may not be criminal offences, but could lead to one.

For regular penitents, little by way of counsel is usually needed, though some will feel cheated if they don't get any and for many, this is the time when they seek spiritual direction. As we have indicated already, counsel should always be to the point and pious remarks should be avoided. When it is given, it should take into account the penitent's condition and so be relevant to their needs and way of life. (See also chapter on *"Some Imaginary Confessions and Suggested Counsel"* at p. 79.)

Acts of Contrition and Penance

The act of contrition is made after the penitent has been given a penance. Due to the considerable number of Anglicans who have in recent years been received into full communion with the Catholic Church and have been used to making their confession, they may need reminding to do this, as for some reason it is not common in Anglican (or at least Church of England) confessionals. Some may need a little reminder on this point.

Acts of contrition vary enormously. The *Rite of Penance* has a large number of examples, but the penitent may use another, perhaps one learned in childhood, perhaps one of his/her own composition. Penitents whose first language is not English may well want to use an Act of Contrition from their mother tongue, which is perfectly acceptable, though some are quite long and may take the new priest by surprise!

The *penance* itself is an integral part of the sacrament and should never be omitted, except, perhaps, in the case of the very sick or dying. It is a token satisfaction and the penitent must indicate his/her assent. This means he/she has understood what has been given and is willing to perform it. There is an apocryphal story told about an elderly deaf penitent who was asked to say Psalm 118 (the longest of the Psalms!). She had not only heard what the priest asked, but she also knew what it was and so she said "Pardon, Father?" He repeated what he had said. Several times she protested that she couldn't hear, so the priest changed the penance to Psalm 150. The penitent accepted with alacrity!

The *Rite of Penance* states: *"The act of penance should serve not only to make up for the past but also help him [i.e. the penitent] begin a new life and provide him with the antidote to weakness. As far as possible, the penance should correspond to the seriousness and nature of the sins. This act of penance may suitably take the form of prayer, self-denial, and especially service of one's neighbour and works of mercy. This will underline the fact that sin and its forgiveness have a social aspect."* Quite a contrast to "Three *Hail Marys*" or "One *Our Father*" which are still quite commonly given. Now, we do have a problem here. Firstly, it is not always easy to produce, on the spot, a penance which "corresponds to the seriousness and nature of the sins", although this should come with practice. Secondly, a penance which is an act of self-denial or service of one's neighbour or a work of mercy is something which the penitent may forget to do, especially if the opportunity does not arise fairly quickly after the confession has been made.

Furthermore, the penitent, instead of leaving the church with that 'walking-on-air' feeling, may leave with the thought of an added burden. Then, when he/she comes to their next confession, there might be an extra sin to confess: "Father, I forgot (or didn't do) my penance after my last confession." Quite understandably, the post-conciliar Church wants its priests to move away from the "Three *Hail Marys*" type of penance, but the penance should always be something that can be performed without too much difficulty. Some, maybe many, priests would say that a penance should be something which can be performed before leaving the church, in which case it would almost always need to be a prayer or a reading.

The challenge is to give something which you can be very certain is known by heart, and those under (say) fifty years of age know very few prayers by heart. Of course, there is always the parish Mass book at the back of the church or even the hymn book, but numbers are often difficult to memorize for the penitent, even given a short space of time, and not everyone is sufficiently familiar with the Mass book to find, e.g, the first reading for last Sunday, or the Gospel for the Twentieth Sunday of the Year, or the

Opening Prayer for Advent II, or the third Preface for
Easter. If you happen to know or recognize your
penitent, it is easier to choose your penance for him
or her. Some priests have lists of written penances
which are numbered and can be handed out in the
confessional. This might be done particularly for
children or young people which may also introduce
them to new prayers. A decade of the rosary is fine for
a life-long Catholic over fifty, but under that age one
cannot guarantee that they will be familiar with the
rosary. If a *"Hail Mary"* is given to a child, it is a good
idea to direct him/her to recite it prayerfully before the
statue or shrine of Our Lady, or if an *"Our Father"*, to
say it in front of the tabernacle.

The *Rite of Penance* says, as we quoted above, that
*"as far as possible, the penance should correspond to
the seriousness and nature of the sins"* and this
certainly needs to be borne in mind, but a penance
should not be complicated and should err on the side
of being light rather than heavy. Keep things in
proportion. In the light of what was suggested above,
it is best that a penance be something that can be
done once and for all and not repeated day after day.
Priests (rarely, one hopes) have been known to set a

penance which lasts to the end of one's life! This is simply *not* acceptable and the penitent has every right to ask for something much lighter (and more practical). If the priest who heard the confession will not change it, then the penitent has every right to go to another priest and ask for it to be commuted.

It is important always to distinguish between *penance* and *counsel*. The penance *must* be performed; the counsel is not mandatory, but a wise penitent will want to follow it. If, e.g., the confessor is helping a penitent to get into the habit of daily personal prayer, then it is *not* helpful to set this as a penance - "Say some prayers every day" - but strongly to *commend* it and give some brief guidance, *is*. The confessor should always make quite clear what is the penance and what is counsel.

CHAPTER VII

RECONCILIATION, FREQUENCY AND SPIRITUAL DIRECTION

Reconciliation, Frequency and Spiritual Direction

It does not take long to discover who are the frequent penitents. There are still those who will come once a week or at least once a fortnight, often with the same few sins, expressed in exactly the same way, usually not serious. Now, such penitents can sometimes be the most difficult to deal with because they do not understand the concept of growth in the Christian life. You may ask them what they are doing to overcome those particular sins that they keep confessing, but it seems to fall on deaf ears. Are they really penitent or do they come out of habit? Perhaps, having made every effort to help them grow, it is best simply to get on with the one thing they have come for and we can give them as priests – forgiveness. There are those penitents who definitely seek spiritual direction when they come to confession and would be disappointed if all they received were a penance. Some of these would like to have a spiritual director and maybe we can suggest one to them. It would probably be fair to say that the majority of "regular" penitents come twice a year – before Christmas and before Easter. They may or may not come to the advertised Penitential Service if their parish has one, but they come very faithfully and regularly. It would be good to encourage greater frequency and so greater growth, but established patterns are not easy to change and at least these penitents are faithful to the Church's teaching and to their own rule.

Many priests do not have a charism to be spiritual directors, though that does not mean that they cannot give spiritual direction and indeed in the confessional can hardly fail to do so. Parish priests in particular may find that they simply have not the time to give formal direction to more than a very few people, who may or may not be their parishioners. Nowadays, there are some good courses in the art of spiritual direction, whose clients are more likely to be religious or lay people than priests and more likely to be women than men. It is important for all concerned to see this ministry as quite separate from that of the confessional, even though there may be a deal of overlap. The good non-ordained spiritual director should know when a directee needs to be encouraged to make his or her confession, just as a confessor should know when a penitent needs to be encouraged to find a spiritual director. But the two ministries are distinct, one being a sacrament, the other not. It is also important that those who seek spiritual direction are never under the illusion that this is a substitute for the Sacrament of Reconciliation. The essence of the Sacrament is always forgiveness of sins, whatever else may accompany it. Its focus must be sin and how to root it out of an individual's life.

So far as frequency of sacramental confession is concerned, a priest must from time to time make clear to his people the Church's rules. As we said earlier, every Catholic is under obligation to confess grave (mortal) sins at least once a year. Every Catholic is also bound to make his or her confession before receiving Holy Communion or another sacrament in the case of a grave (mortal) sin. However, many practising Catholics rarely if ever commit a grave sin, but during the course of a week (even a day) may accumulate many lesser sins. These impede Christian growth and weaken resistance to sin generally, even making the possibility of grave sin more likely. So every Catholic should be encouraged to come to the sacrament more frequently than once or even twice a year. A wise confessor will help a penitent to increase the frequency by realistic and encouraging counsel.

Relation of the Sacrament of Reconciliation to the other sacraments

The *Catechism of the Catholic Church* places both Reconciliation and the Sacrament of the Sick under the heading of *The Sacraments of Healing*, thus reflecting the way in which Jesus in the Gospels would often, when asked to heal someone physically or mentally, also specifically forgive them their sins, (e.g. *Mark* 2:1-12). This helps us to see forgiveness of sin in the light of a person being made whole. Sometimes, of course, sin and sickness are directly related. Both sickness and sinfulness reveal human vulnerability.

But Reconciliation is also closely related to Baptism and is, in a sense, that part of Baptism which can and needs to be repeated, *viz.* the remission of sins, in the case of an adult being baptized. One analogy for baptism is of a branch or shoot being grafted onto a tree or vine. It takes on the life of that tree or vine and the sap begins to flow through it. But, as Jesus tells us in John 15, a branch that bears no fruit has to be pruned and even branches that do bear fruit have to pruned in order to be more productive. If grafting is a good analogy for baptism, then pruning is a good analogy for the Sacrament of Reconciliation. It gets us away from the "laundry" type of analogy which can be too negative.

But Reconciliation is very much linked to the sacrament of the Holy Eucharist. Any one who has sinned gravely may not receive Holy Communion until they have made their confession – been reconciled with God and neighbour. This aspect of Church teaching needs particular emphasis today when so many approach the altar not only without the sacramental absolution they require, but without even knowing they require it. Such teaching must, of course, be set in the context of God's love and our relationship with him.

In a word, of course, Reconciliation is the sacrament that prepares us for all the others, with the exception of Baptism. Those preparing for First Holy Communion, for Full Communion with the Church (which includes Confirmation), candidates for

Confirmation at whatever age, couples (or at least the Catholic member) for Matrimony, candidates for Holy Orders, are all expected to celebrate the Sacrament of Reconciliation just before the event.

CHAPTER VIII

SOME IMAGINARY CONFESSIONS AND SUGGESTED COUNSEL

SOME IMAGINARY CONFESSIONS AND SUGGESTED COUNSEL

The following are exactly what the title states – *imaginary* confessions and suggested counsel. The purpose is to set out a range of ages and conditions of men, women, young people and children, with some of the sins which you might hear from each. There is no such thing as a "typical confession" and you must always prepare to be surprised – but not shocked. As for the counsel, remember that the Holy Spirit is very much present in the confessional and so what is suggested is given in broad brush strokes only. In most cases, you will never need or feel it right to comment on every sin confessed.

Penitent: Middle-aged family man

My last confession was six months ago at Easter. During that time I've missed Sunday Mass a few times, sometimes when I've been away and sometimes because we've been out for the day as a family and haven't got back in time for the evening Mass.
I lied to my wife once.

I've been mad with the children, usually when they have misbehaved, but sometimes when it hasn't been their fault and I've just felt tired.

I've been lazy at home and left things to my wife which I should have done.

I've not been good at saying my prayers regularly.

I gave one of my staff a hard time when he slipped up over some figures.

I think that's all, Father – oh yes, I once looked at a pornographic site on the internet – not for long, but long enough to arouse sexual fantasies.

Comment: This is a "good" confession on the part of a man who does try to live the faith. You may want to question him about the lie to his wife – he hasn't indicated how serious it was. You should warn him about the internet, but don't come down heavily because clearly his encounter with the site was brief and he is aware of the danger. After that, you could take one other matter confessed. You might, for example, want to encourage him with his prayer, gently question what he means by not being regular, see whether he needs some constructive counsel. Or you might choose his relationship with his children or his wife. He is probably a man with a very responsible job and comes home fairly exhausted.

Penitent: Young woman in her twenties

I think my last confession was last Christmas – anyway about a year ago.

I've gossiped a lot at work about a girl that nobody likes. I've been rude to my Mum who still treats me like a child. I've slept with my boyfriend, but I don't really think it's wrong because we are in love.

Comment: We have to be thankful that this young woman still comes to confession. It may not be very thorough, but it contains very serious matter about which counsel is required. You will need to give some clear teaching about extra-marital sex without being heavy-handed and insensitive. This woman is questioning the Church's teaching, not dismissing it, otherwise she wouldn't have mentioned the sin at all. Provided you can convince her that she has indeed sinned and that she will do all she can to avoid it in the future, then you can give absolution. You might notice she has said nothing about prayer and although you cannot raise this directly, you might ask whether she prays about any of the sins she has confessed.

Penitent: Middle-aged, unmarried woman

It's a month since my last confession and I remember these sins:

I missed Mass on a Holyday because I was on holiday and there was no Catholic church near by.

I've been judgemental and criticized some of my colleagues at work for their life-styles and attitudes.

I've neglected to visit my mother as often as I should. Now that she's in a home, she relies on my visits more than ever.

I was rude to a "cold caller" on the 'phone the other evening.

I haven't been a very good example of a Christian and sometimes wonder what difference my faith makes to my life.

Comment: Here is a faithful Catholic woman who is well aware of her faults and needs some encouragement. Explain that to be aware of not being as good a Christian example as one would like to be, is a healthy sign and that she probably does better than she thinks. However, she could be encouraged to look at various areas of her life to see where the light of Christ might shine more brightly.

Penitent: Elderly, widowed man

It must be quite a few weeks since I last came.

I know I should have come before.

I've used my age as an excuse for not getting to Mass every Sunday.

I've always had a temper, Father, and last week I swore at the children next door when their ball came over my fence and hit my greenhouse.

I've committed some impure acts on my own a few times.

I meant to write to a friend of mine when his wife died, but I never got around to it and I never got to the funeral.

Comment: This man has thought out his confession, giving clear facts and circumstances. You may like to ask him if a lift to Mass would be of help. He has probably mentioned his bad temper hundreds of times before and he has doubtless heard every bit of advice that he could possibly receive. However, this is an opportunity for him to hear your counsel. Has he ever tried laughing at himself for being a grumpy old man?

Penitent: Child before First Communion

This is my First Confession and I remember these sins:

I have disobeyed my parents.

I have hit my brother.

Comment: It is not unknown for parents to tell their children what to say, but this one is probably the child's own work. (*See section on Hearing Children's Confessions, p. 95.*). You will probably find that this is a very typical confession for a child of seven or eight or even older. You might remind the little boy or girl that Jesus was once his/her age and didn't always find it easy to do what his parents asked him to do, though he always did it because he loved them and he loved his Father in heaven. The point is that our Lord understands us when we do wrong though he is sorry that we do, but he helps us, if we let him, to do better next time. If you gently question about hitting the brother, you may discover that the brother is considerably older and may have been teasing the child. On the other hand, he may be younger and had broken one of his/her toys. It is unlikely that we have the beginnings of a violent offender!

Penitent: Young teenage boy

I've been lazy.

I've not listened to my Mum.

I've answered back to my teachers, especially one who is always getting at me.

I haven't done my homework.

I've helped give a boy in my class a hard time and laughed when he cried.

Comment: The boy may be one of your altar servers who comes pretty regularly to Mass. There is no mention of prayer, so you might ask if he's ever thought of praying about some of the things he has confessed. The last sin, neatly wrapped up in that phrase "hard time", is about bullying, but the penitent has probably not initiated it, yet found himself drawn into it, afraid to stand aside or speak out against it. Give him some help and encouragement to do those things if he can, tough though it may be. Explain that God gives the grace through prayer and Holy Communion. Here is an opportunity to do a little teaching about sacramental life and daily living.

Penitent: Young teenage girl

I've fallen out with my best friend.

I've sent her texts which were out of order.

I told a lie to one of my teachers to get out of trouble.

I've used bad language.

I said I didn't want to see my Dad last Saturday because I wanted to meet my friends.

Comment: Falling out with friends is very common with teenage girls and is not necessarily a sin. They often make it up in a few days. The second sin is not, of course, about mixing up the pages of a photocopied document! We all need to know our "street-speak" these days. The penitent has sent some (probably) unpleasant (or worse) messages on her mobile, again quite common with girls of this age. Has she apologized? She should. Did the lie to the teacher involve someone else being accused or punished? Be specially gentle over the last sin. So many of our children are compelled by law to see a parent, usually a father, who has left the mother. She might be glad to talk about the situation and while you may sympathize, especially if she feels resentful about the father leaving the home and even more so if he has a girlfriend or has married again, help her to understand that he still loves her and wants to see her. This is where sacramental confession and pastoral counselling overlap. N.B. - We mentioned above the need for a confessor to be familiar with contemporary "street-speak". Any attempt to give a glossary of some of these could be self-defeating as language, especially with the young, changes so rapidly these days. For example, the young teenage boy, above, who "answered back" his teachers might well say he "dissed" them, i.e. was disrespectful to them, but this word could be archaic by next year, if it is not already! The word "wicked" meaning exactly the opposite, has been in vogue for some time now, but may soon be on the wane. A priest who goes into his school(s) should listen carefully to the language of the young people and ask if he does not understand it. Adults, too, can raise difficulties by using unfamiliar euphemisms concerning their sins. If you do not understand, then ask.

Penitent:A priest

My last confession was a month ago.
I have omitted to say Evening Prayer on two occasions – once when I mislaid my Office book and once when I simply forgot, as my routine was rather different that day due to a pastoral emergency.

I have sometimes said Mass rather mechanically.

I have omitted some pastoral visits, especially one to a sick parishioner.

I've rather neglected my elderly parents and failed at least to phone them regularly. I got very angry with a parishioner who applied late for the First Communion programme but insisted that her child joined it.

I failed once to turn off the TV when I found the programme was arousing me sexually.

Comment: This is almost certainly a conscientious and faithful priest who comes regularly to confession and probably needs to hear an encouraging word. You might want to ask if he normally makes some preparation before he says Mass, as this can help avoid being mechanical in one's celebration. Encourage him to keep in more regular contact with his parents and perhaps make some time to visit them, even if this means leaving aside some parish work. It is particularly tempting when hearing a priest's confession to collude with some of his sins. One may draw from one's own experience of overcoming a particular temptation or dealing with a particular fault, but one must be as objective as possible.

Penitent: Police officer (middle-aged man)

It's ages since I've been to confession, Father, but there's one thing been troubling me for a few years.

I once gave false evidence which caused an innocent man to be sent to prison.

He's due out soon and I suppose this is why I'm specially worried.

I've not always been a good husband to my wife and I've sometimes been stricter than I need have done with the children.

I've made my Sunday duties an excuse for not getting to Mass when I know that, with effort, I could have made one of the Masses sometimes.

I've often used bad language, even at home sometimes.

I know I've been prejudiced at work and judged people by the colour of their skin.

There must be lots of other things, Father, but they are all I can remember just now.

Comment: This is the kind of confession that makes you want to rejoice and weep at the same time. The Holy Spirit has brought this man back to confession after a long time and it is worth saying that to him.

Commend him on his courage. But the first sin he confessed is very serious – as serious as we are likely to hear. You might question him gently as to the circumstances of his giving false evidence. Was he under duress from others? Was it because he simply did not like this defendant, or because he thought he was guilty and so wanted him convicted, but knew the clear evidence was too slim? He must be encouraged to make a full confession to his superiors and take the consequences. You could say that if he is truly penitent, then he will, even though the consequences will be felt by his family. He said in his confession that he is already worried about the consequences of the innocent man being released – fear of a reprisal of some kind? Of course, that is something he might have to face in any case, but does he feel that by confessing God might spare him that? As a confessor, we must always put the best construction on why someone comes and not concern ourselves excessively with motives. The only other matter you might comment on is his relationship with his wife. Does it mean he forgot her birthday once or more times, or does it mean he has had relationships with other women? You might feel it right to impose a heavy penance, but in the circumstances, this is unnecessary. Trying to pluck up courage to do what you have advised will be hard enough. Do assure him of the Church's pastoral support whatever happens.

Penitent: Middle-aged mother

My last confession was at Easter, I think (*i.e. a few months ago*).

I feel a complete failure, Father. All my three children are living with partners. None of them go to Mass. One is pregnant and I'm worried she won't have the baby baptized. My husband says this is the modern world and we have to get used to it. We often argue about this and then we stop speaking for a while. He used to be such a good Catholic, but says the Church is out of date and not much use to him.

I've gossiped at work about colleagues and haven't stood up for my faith when issues have come up.

I try to remember my prayers each day, but am often distracted when I pray.

I found a pornographic magazine in my husband's jacket when I took it to the cleaner's and destroyed it. Did I do right, Father?

I have sometimes driven the car carelessly and once

did some damage to it. My husband was furious and said he wouldn't let me drive it if it happened again.

Comment: Here is a truly troubled penitent who obviously lives with a dominant husband. Assure her that she did right to destroy the magazine. As for her children, she is far from being alone, as we know too well. Assure her that she is not a "failure" as a parent. After all, we are God's children, but still choose too often to go our own way. As long as she continues to love her children but in no way condones their life-style, they may one day return to the values with which they were brought up. What about the husband? Does she pray for him? When an argument begins again, suggest that it would be better if they simply agreed to differ. But you might also suggest that she try standing up for herself when he behaves in an aggressive manner. You might say something like this: "It sounds as though you have rather a tough time in your marriage. Do you ever talk things over with your husband so that he knows how you feel?" So far as the penitent's prayer is concerned, you may want to reassure her that distractions in prayer are extremely common, but it can help if she will spend a little time settling into prayer.

CHAPTER IX

HEARING CHILDREN'S CONFESSIONS

HEARING CHILDREN'S CONFESSIONS

The first confession a child makes will normally be before his or her First Communion. However well the child has been catechized by the catechist and, let us trust, his or her parent(s), do not be surprised if he/she either seizes up or seems very nervous and uncertain. Patience, gentleness and kindness are paramount. For some, the nervousness may express itself in such a way that the child will seem not to be taking the Sacrament seriously. These days, of course, many of the children will come from non-practising homes and even the church building may be a somewhat alien environment, though to be fair, some priests will only admit to the First Communion programme those whose families are practising their faith. A priest should ask the catechists to do all they can to encourage the Catholic parent (or both, if Catholics), to make their confession at the same time as the child. It is best to let all the children come first and then the parents and indeed, why not the catechists, too?

Some parishes try to make sure that their First Communicants come to confession more than once before their First Communion. For example, if the First Confession is before Christmas, the second can be before Easter (this may happen during Lent in a Catholic primary school) and a third just before the First Communion itself. Indeed, it would seem rather important that each child *should* confess just before this great celebration in their lives. In this way, the children become more accustomed to the Sacrament of Reconciliation. Unfortunately, for not a few children, their second confession will not be until just before their Confirmation, if indeed they get that far.

Some, if not all, dioceses have their own guidelines for hearing children's confessions (quite apart from protection issues) and so it is important to have a copy of these and be familiar with them. It is important to remember that even if there are regular Services of Reconciliation in the primary school, not all those in the parish (especially if parts of it are in rural areas) attend a Catholic school and, of course, there are rural parishes where there is no Catholic school. A parish priest may wish to arrange a separate Service of Reconciliation for children – and their parents - in the church before, say, Christmas and Easter, maybe after school or at the week-end. The communal aspect of *Rite II* may help to encourage them, rather than hope that they will come to the advertised *Rite I* celebrations. Incidentally, provision should always be made for children (as for adults) to choose whether they wish to confess behind the grille or face-to-face. Even when temporary confessionals are set up to accommodate extra confessors and there is no actual grille, there should be the possibility for the penitent to kneel alongside the priest so that there is no visual contact.

Many priests will know the experience of hearing confessions in a Catholic secondary school and discovering how a young person will not remember when he or she last celebrated the Sacrament – more than likely, if it is a Year Seven student, it will have been before their First Communion. One does not want to give too gloomy a picture, as we must all know good Catholic families where the children come regularly (even frequently) with their parents to the Sacrament.

Perhaps a word or two about catechizing children for the Sacrament needs to be added. It has been known for a catechist not to make it absolutely clear to the child that he or she is coming to the Sacrament in order to confess *sin*, however that word is defined. The essential grace of the Sacrament is God's forgiveness. Even though the priest may speak some helpful words, the words of absolution, as we well know, are the essential ones and it is primarily for that reason – God's forgiveness - that anyone, child or adult, celebrates the Sacrament. To try and wrap this up in therapeutic language, as sometimes happens, is both unhelpful and misleading, to say the least.

It is obviously of enormous help if, before first confessions are heard, the children are shown the confessional and any other point in the church where confessions take place. If a priest could be present, vested in his stole, and demonstrate what will happen, this will go a long way towards alleviating fears. The priest may also say something like this: "*I* have to go to confession, too, you know – so does the Bishop, yes, and even the Pope. We all do wrong things and need God's loving forgiveness." If the children have been properly catechized then they will know that making one's confession is not about punishment (they may or may not have been punished by teachers or parents for what they are going to confess). The penance is not meant as a punishment, any more than the process of confessing. It is about receiving God's loving forgiveness and this should be emphasized.

Arrangements for children's confessions, following the *Nolan* and *Cumberledge Reports*, need to be given special attention. Quoting from the document *"Safe and Sound"*: "The sacrament of reconciliation for children should wherever possible be administered in a setting where both priest and child can be seen but not heard." But note also: "It is clearly not possible to give detailed procedures for this. Each priest and parish will need to work out the most appropriate arrangement for the accommodation available to them." One might add also that to avoid any possibility of lip-reading, the penitent's face (child or adult) should not be seen. Any doubts about the arrangements for hearing children's confessions should be addressed to the Child Protection Officer of one's diocese. As always, the priest needs protection as well as the penitent. Although it is highly unlikely that a child will be making his or her confession when no one else is present in the church, there is always the slight possibility that a parent might slip out of church to attend to some other matter. Parents should therefore be asked, perhaps from time to time in the parish newsletter, to stay in the main body of the church until their child leaves the confessional. A priest left alone in a church with a child, especially in a confessional, could risk being open to false accusations.

(N.B. All that has just been said applies equally to the confessions of vulnerable adults.)

CHAPTER X

CONFESSIONS OF THE DYING

CONFESSIONS OF THE DYING

One of the best examples of the classic death-bed repentance is to be found in Evelyn Waugh's *Brideshead Revisited*, but few priests will encounter this nowadays, not least because so many dying people are under heavy sedation.

The best time to encourage someone to make what may well be their last confession is when they are coming to the end, so far as the doctors can tell, of a terminal illness but are still conscious (obviously). This is not always easy to judge and the question needs to be put very sensitively. Relatives are not always very helpful in this respect and some may be hostile to the priest's ministry anyway. We may well have had instances of a deceased Catholic not even being allowed a Catholic funeral. In one sense confessions of the dying are no different from any other confessions. The rite is the same, though would no doubt be reduced to the minimum and the priest may suggest saying both the act of contrition and the penance with the penitent.

Remember that the Apostolic Pardon may also be given to the dying at the end of the *Rite of Penance* (or the Penitential Rite if the dying person does not make sacramental confession).

One may also give Holy Communion at the same time if the patient is able to receive and this may well be their Viaticum. A priest may occasionally witness a serious (e.g. road) accident or a "major incident" (e.g. a terrorist bombing, natural disaster, train crash, fire, explosion). On these occasions, as so often in the case of the dying at home or in hospital, he can only administer conditional absolution. It goes without saying that a dying person is unlikely to be able to make a full confession of sins, even of all unconfessed grave sins, and so the conditions in this respect and in others must be waived in case of death. The one thing the priest *must* do is to ensure the secrecy of the seal and so must ask for others present to leave the room or move out of earshot.

One of the problems a priest sometimes faces these days is the lack of understanding on the part of the nursing and medical profession as to the ministry of a priest. Most, if not all, are co-operative and not a few are very appreciative, especially if they know he has come out in the middle of the night. It is always worth remembering how much weight the Church puts upon the need and opportunity for the sacraments when a person is *in extremis*, even to the extent of any priest inhibited from exercising his ministry being not only allowed, but obliged to minister the sacraments to the dying.

CHAPTER XI

SERVICES OF RECONCILIATION

SERVICES OF RECONCILIATION

As is clear from the Introduction to the *Rite of Penance*, there are three possible forms:

A. The Rite for the Reconciliation of Individual Penitents, i.e. with no assembly for a service of the Word and preparation;

B. The Rite for Reconciliation of Several Penitents with Individual Confession and Absolution, i.e. an assembly with a short liturgy of the Word including time and opportunity in silence for examination of conscience; and

C. Rite for the Reconciliation of Penitents with General Confession and Absolution. This last is for very exceptional circumstances and is very clearly set out in the Introduction § 31-35.

However, there have been instances of this rite (C) being used when it is quite unjustified and also instances of Rite B being abused. For example, penitents have been invited to confess three or fewer sins only, or to write out their sins and show them to the confessor. This is strictly forbidden (cf *Misericordia Dei*, § 3). A sacramental confession must be a full confession of all grave sins and it must also be oral. A penitent may want to make notes as a *vade mecum* before going into the confessional, but they are for his/her own eyes only.

Some parishes find that the majority of their penitents come to a Service of Reconciliation, which would normally take place before Christmas and Easter, though may happen at other appropriate times. However, it is important that other opportunities for individual confession in the normal way be advertised. *Priests must make it as easy as possible for people to celebrate the Sacrament. (Misericordia Dei § 2).* Parish priests within a deanery might often invite one another to hear confessions in their churches at one or more of these advertised times and not only for a Service of Reconciliation, especially before Christmas and Easter, and to advertise the fact. One has to face the fact that not all parishioners want to go to their parish priest, especially if they work closely with him in ministry or administration or, dare one say it, they have fallen out with him and wish to confess their part in that.

There are clear directions in the *Rite of Penance* for penitential celebrations (§ 36-37), but it is worth noting what may help or hinder. During the time for self-examination it can help to have the Blessed Sacrament exposed. But it is probably best to avoid hymn singing during the time that confessions are being heard as it can be very distracting. It puts penitent and confessor under great stress trying to listen to one another if, e.g., the strains of *Bind us together, Lord* are filling every nook and cranny of the church!

However, soft music and gentle music can be helpful, especially in respect of avoiding overhearing, particularly when several provisional confessionals are being used.

CHAPTER XII

WHEN ABSOLUTION SHOULD BE WITHHELD

When Absolution should be Withheld

Rarely! This needs to be said first of all. But we have to remember the words of our Lord: "whosoever sins you retain, they are retained." In order to receive forgiveness, one must have committed and confessed a sin, as was noted in an earlier section. The priest in the confessional does have the role of a judge and must know when and to whom absolution should be either conferred, refused or deferred. *Rit. Rom. III c. xii* states: "Moreover the priest must take into consideration when absolution may be given, when and to whom it must be denied or deferred, for fear that he give absolution to those who refuse to lay aside quarrels and enmities, who refuse to make such restitution as is possible, who refuse to abandon a proximate occasion of sin, or to give up their sins in some other way and amend their lives, or such have given public scandal without making public restitution and thus removing the scandal." A penitent to whom absolution should be denied is one who is clearly impenitent, showing no signs of sorrow; who refuses to set aside what is causing scandal.

A priest must always assume an intention of amendment here and now unless there is clear evidence to the contrary. For example, a priest may ask a penitent to avoid the occasion of a certain sin if this can be done voluntarily. He may advise the abandonment of remote occasions, but he can require the abandonment of neither remote occasions nor necessary proximate occasions – only of voluntary proximate occasions. A proximate occasion is necessary if, for instance, it is required by the penitent's established state of life, employment or public duty.

Some occasions, of course, are more proximate than others A fully proximate occasion is one from which sin (for this penitent at any rate) almost invariably results: a determination not to abandon it implies a lack of repentance. If sin sometimes or even frequently results, the confessor may advise its abandonment. Take the following as an example. A penitent confesses to frequent drunkenness. The proximate occasions are social gatherings with other heavy drinkers. They are voluntary if they consist of visits to certain public houses or clubs, or visits to them with certain particular friends. However, if the penitent be, let us say, a public relations officer, and the occasions are business lunches or dinners which he must attend or lose his job, they are necessary proximate occasions and not voluntary. Some other way must be adopted for dealing with the sin. These days, if one has driven to the event rather than have taken a taxi, there is an added incentive to keep off alcohol – not only because one could easily go over the limit and break the law (a crime), but because one might cause someone's death or injury (a crime and a sin).

Making restitution is a more obvious business. If, for example, a penitent has stolen some money, he can hardly be said to repent if he has no intention of returning it. But the restitution asked for must be possible. If the penitent no longer has the money, he may not be able to raise it without causing intolerable hardship to others, such as dependents, but "intolerable hardship" is not the same thing as "some inconvenience".

He may, however, be able to return it over a period of time. In cases where the theft has been undiscovered, the restitution can only be required if it can be done without discovery. Where a very small sum of money is concerned, confessors usually suggest that the penitent give the same amount to some charity.

Where such a thing as public scandal is concerned, then the restitution needs to be public. One of the most common situations today is that of cohabiting, which can create a very real problem for the confessor. In the case of a man and woman, neither of whom has been married and no children are involved, counsel is relatively straightforward. They must cease to have sexual intercourse and if they are truly in love and there are no impediments, they should be urged to marry as soon as possible. It may be unrealistic to tell them (or rather, the party who is currently the penitent), to live apart, as one of them may immediately become homeless. If they do not intend to marry, then they should make plans to live apart. (But be aware that there are rare instances of a man and woman living under the same roof as close friends, but never having sexual relations).

In the case of a man and woman cohabiting, one or both of whom have a spouse still living, the situation is more complicated. Sad to say, this is not uncommon today and no longer constitutes – outside the Church at any rate – what could be called a "public scandal". If either party repents, then repentance requires separation. But they may have produced a family, one may be financially dependent upon the other, their former spouse or spouses may have re-married or be themselves cohabiting and therefore return to the marital home would be impossible. If this new (and it may not be very "new") relationship is stable, then there is the possibility of seeking an annulment, but which may not be granted. All this is difficult to deal with in the confines of the confessional and is an example of where a priest may invite the penitent to a pastoral counselling session still under the seal ("A chat in the presbytery as soon as possible"). In all cases of cohabitation, if the penitent refuses to cease a physical relationship with the cohabitee until the cohabitation has been regularized (if indeed it can be), then absolution must be refused *and the implications of this for the other sacraments made clear.* The latter, of course, applies to all situations where absolution has to be refused.

With regard to the sin of using artificial contraception in a marriage, the reader is directed to the *Vademecum for Confessors concerning some aspects of the morality of conjugal life* (Pontifical Council for the Family, 1997, pub. Libreria Editrice Vaticana), where the whole matter is dealt with fully.

What about quarrels and enmities? There must be a promise to lay these aside, but not necessarily to make them up (though obviously that would be good), for absolution to be given. Satisfaction may involve the penitent in an apology, if an insult has been clear and explicit.

In cases - and they are rare – where absolution has to be refused, the reason for it should be made clear: the penitent is professing to be repentant but refusing penance and satisfaction. What about the vexed question of recidivism? Admittedly, this is often a bigger problem for the penitent than for the confessor and penitents will sometimes say: "I'm afraid it's the same old sins, Father." The wise confessor will say: "Well, be thankful it's not lots of new ones!" But having begun in this light-hearted way, he may then give whatever counsel seems appropriate. But when it is a more serious matter than, say, being short-tempered, the matter needs sensitive handling. On the one hand, the confessor does not want to make the penitent think that he/she had better not come back with this sin again, however bad, as this could lead to sacrilegious confessions or a falling away from the Sacrament altogether. On the other hand, a penitent needs help and encouragement to fight the temptation which leads to the sin. But if the sin is fast becoming a compulsive habit and therefore resistant to direct means of dealing with it, another approach is needed.

Sometimes, it is right simply to ignore the sin altogether when giving counsel, at other times to counsel avoiding the proximate or remote occasions. Genuinely compulsive habits are diseases rather than formal sins, though they may well have originated in properly voluntary sins. As St Basil says in *Moralia xxiii*: "He who is drawn away by sin against his will ought to understand that he is being mastered by some other previous sin which he served willingly, and is henceforward led under its power even to things which he does not wish". Examples of such compulsive habits would be: alcoholism, masturbation and lying. The guilt and therefore the contrition of the sinner may be genuine, but not in fact related to the matter, or some of the matter confessed. The confessor is certainly a physician of souls, but not in order to diagnose the psychological causes of drives and urges, but to distinguish between guilt and a false sense of guilt, so fixing the guilt in the right place. As we have said elsewhere, there may be occasions when the confessor will suggest professional counselling or therapy. Even if the priest is qualified in this respect (and some are), the confessional is not the place to practise it and the penitent must exercise complete freedom both as to whether to follow the suggestion and from whom to accept the therapy.

Chapter XIII

The Sacrament of Reconciliation, Counselling and Therapy

THE SACRAMENT OF RECONCILIATION, COUNSELLING AND THERAPY

Over fifty years ago, Fr Victor White, O.P. wrote a book entitled *God and the Unconscious* and in his chapter "The Analyst and the Confessor" he sets out a description of the roles of the two, making a clear distinction between them, but at the same time showing how each can be of help to the other. Therapeutic medicine has moved on a great deal since those days, of course, but the basic distinction between analyst and confessor remains. Fr White points out that the analyst who plays the confessor will be as bad an analyst as the confessor who plays the analyst will be a bad confessor. The significant difference is this. Basically, what will happen in analysis will be uncharted territory with no ready-made maps even though there may be compasses. All will be determined by the material which emerges in the analysis itself. By contrast, the Sacrament of Penance has over the centuries acquired a structure and its ingredients are formulated. The "remote matter" of the Sacrament is sins committed since baptism or the penitent's last confession – the evil that human beings do. The "remote matter" of analysis is a sickness, an evil that human beings suffer – involuntary and contrary to the sufferer's will. In what ways can each help the other? Well, here is just one example. Sacramental confession may do much to prevent the disorders with which psychotherapy is concerned. Psychotherapy, on the other hand, may do much to free a patient from some of those compulsions we mentioned in a previous chapter which are often so difficult for a penitent to deal with. Divine grace which is at work in the Sacrament can also function through therapy, depending upon the patient's response to that grace. It might help to set out the focus of the various forms of help for both psychic and spiritual health.

Psychic health

First, *Therapy*, whose client is a disordered patient needing healing. The need is for a resolution of psychic conflict leading to a more adjusted life. Various forms of professional help are available for this.

Secondly, *Counselling*, whose client is troubled, needing help at a time of crisis, seeking the solution of a problem. He/she needs help in coping with life by seeing things in proportion and clarifying options. A skilled professional counsellor is needed.

Thirdly, *Pastoral Counselling*, which has the same focus as Counselling but with an added faith dimension. A priest, pastor, lay or ordained, with spiritual depth and empathy should be sought. But Pastoral Counselling could equally come under the heading of:

Spiritual health

Here is included also *Spiritual Direction*, which is sought by a Christian who wishes to deepen his/her relationship with God, wanting a greater integration of faith with life, leading to ever greater freedom of spirit. Such a person needs to be open to the Spirit and be prepared to surrender to God and discern his will in his/her life. A spiritual director may be lay or ordained and should be a guide of sufficient empathy and spiritual awareness, and if possible have had some training in this ministry.

And finally, the *Sacrament of Reconciliation* available for all Catholic Christians, who are also urged to celebrate it regularly. In this Sacrament the penitent seeks God's loving forgiveness, which should lead to spiritual growth and conversion of heart. The confessor must be an ordained priest or bishop.

In conclusion, we can only repeat what was said above and that is that a confessor, who may borrow insights from psychology, counselling and psychotherapy (not least, good listening skills) must never allow the Sacrament of Penance to become other than what it is – the God-given means of forgiving a penitent all his/her sins in the name of and through the power of Christ, given in ordination.

Censures

Very occasionally, a confessor will encounter a penitent who confesses a sin which carries an inflicted or declared penalty which cannot be remitted in the Sacrament of Penance by the typical confessor, except in danger of death. Such sins are clearly stated in Canon Law, but for completeness, we state them here.

I Automatic Censures (*Latae Sententiae*)

These may incur excommunication, interdict or suspension.

A. Excommunication

Canon Law states that the penalty of excommunication is incurred automatically upon commission of any of the following:

1. Apostasy, heresy, schism (Canon 1364 § 1)

2. Violation of the consecrated species of the Eucharist (Canon 1367)

3. Physical attack on the Pope (Canon 1370 § 1)

4. Absolution of an accomplice in a sin against the sixth commandment (Canon 1378)

5. Unauthorized ordination of a bishop (Canon 1382)

6. Direct violation by a confessor of the seal of confession (Canon 1388)

7. Procuring an abortion (Canon 1398)

8. By means of a technical instrument, recording or divulging in the communications media what was said by a confessor or a penitent in a sacramental confession, whether performed by oneself or by another. (CDF, decree *Urbis et Orbis*, Sept. 23, 1988, AAS 80 (1988) 1367). This penalty refers to the use of a tape recorder or similar device used to record the voice of the confessor or the penitent and then divulged to the media.

N.B. The remission of nos. 2-6 is reserved to the Apostolic See.

B. Interdict

Commission of any of the following results in the penalty of automatic interdict:

1. Physical attack on a bishop

2. Pretended celebration of the Eucharist by a non-priest (Canon 1378 § 42)

3. Attempt to impart sacramental absolution or hear confession by one who cannot do so validly (Canon 1378 § 2, 2)

4. False accusation of the crime of solicitation in the confessional (Canon 1390 § 1)

5. Attempted marriage, even civil, by a religious in perpetual vows (Canon 1394 § 2)

N.B. The crimes mentioned in nos. 2 and 3 result in automatic suspension, in addition to interdict, if the offender is a cleric. Those in nos. 1 and 4 result in both automatic interdict and suspension if the offender is a cleric.

C. Suspension

In addition to those who commit the sins mentioned in nos. 1-4 under Interdict, the following also incur automatic suspension:

1. A cleric who attempts marriage, even civil (Canon 1394 § 1)

2. A cleric who is ordained by a bishop who does not have legitimate dimissorial letters. The suspension affects only the order received illicitly, not a prior order received lawfully (Canon 1383)

II Effects of Automatic Censures

A. Excommunication

The excommunicate is prohibited from:

1. Having any ministerial participation in the celebration of the Eucharist or any other ceremonies of worship

2. Celebrating the sacraments or sacramentals and receiving the sacraments

3. Exercising any ecclesiastical offices, ministries, or functions, or placing acts of governance (Canon 1331 § 1)

B. Interdict

The interdicted is prohibited from nos. 1 and 2 under A (Canon 1332)

C. Suspension

Suspension, which affects only clerics, prohibits:

1. All acts of the power of order

2. All acts of the power of governance

3. The exercise of all rights or functions connected with an office (Canon 1334 § 2)

N.B. The cleric who is automatically suspended as a result of illicit ordination by a bishop lacking dimissorial letters (Canon 1383) is prohibited only from exercising that order, not a lower order licitly received, or acts of the power of governance, or rights, or functions connected with an office.

D. Exceptions to Observance of Censures

If a censure prohibits the celebration of sacraments or sacramentals or placing of an act of governance, the prohibition is suspended whenever it is necessary to provide for the faithful who are in danger of death. If it is an automatic censure which has not been declared, the prohibition is moreover suspended whenever the faithful request a sacrament or sacramental or an act of governance. They make this request for any just reason at all. (Canon 1335)

If the penalty forbids the reception of the sacraments or sacramentals, the prohibition is suspended as long as the person in question is in danger of death. The obligation of observing an automatic penalty, which has not been declared and is not notorious in the place where the offender is living, is suspended totally or partially insofar as the offender is unable to observe it without the danger of grave scandal of infamy. (Canon 1352)

III Those subject to Penalties

In general, those subject to the law are subject to a penalty if they break the law, with the exceptions noted below. A penalty binds personally, not territorially, and therefore remains in effect wherever one goes until it is remitted. (Canon 11-13)

A penalty cannot be incurred or inflicted unless the delict be perfectly executed according to the strict letter of the law. Laws which establish a penalty are subject to strict interpretation. (Canon 18)

Whoever does or omits anything in attempting to commit a crime but, contrary to his or her desire, has not completed the crime, is not bound to the penalty attached by law to the completed crime, unless a law or precept should state otherwise (Canon 1328, § 1; see also 1328, § 2). No one is punished unless the external violation of the law or precept committed by that person is gravely imputable to him or her by reason of malice or culpability. One is bound to the penalty established by a law or precept if that person deliberately violates the law or precept. If the violation occurs as a result of a lack of due diligence the person is not punished, unless the law or precept states otherwise. If the violation is external, imputability is presumed, unless it should appear otherwise. (Canon 1321)

Those who habitually lack the use of reason, even if they seem to have been of sound mind when they violated a law or precept, are considered incapable of committing a crime. (Canon 1322)

If a law has changed after a crime is committed, that law is to be applied, whether the earlier one or later, which is the more favourable to the offender. If the later law abolishes the earlier one, or at least the penalty connected with it, the penalty ceases immediately. (Canon 1313)

Accomplices who are not named in a law or precept incur an automatic penalty connected with an offence if the offence would not have been committed without their efforts and the penalty is of such a nature that it is able to affect them. Otherwise they can be punished by inflicted penalties. (Canon 1329, § 2)

A Summary of Sins and Censures reserved to the Apostolic See

By the Motu Proprio *Sacramentorum Sanctitatis Tutela* of April 30th 2001, Pope John Paul II promulgated norms for more serious delicts reserved to the Congregation of the Faith. Summary as follows:

1. The excommunication incurred from the desecration of the consecrated Eucharistic species. (Canon 1367, *de delictis gravioribus*)

2. The excommunication incurred from using physical force against the Roman Pontiff. (Canon 1370).

3. The excommunication of a priest who violated Canon 977 by attempting to absolve an accomplice of a sin against the sixth commandment except in danger of death. (Canon 1378 § 1, *de delictis gravioribus*)

4. The excommunication of one who is not a priest who attempts to celebrate Mass or of anyone who pretends to celebrate the Eucharistic Sacrifice. (*Canons 1378, § 2 1o, 1379, de delictis gravioribus*)

5. The excommunication incurred by a bishop who ordains another bishop without a pontifical mandate and also incurred by the one ordained. (Canon 1382)

6. The excommunication incurred from the direct violation of the seal of confession. (Canon 1388, § 1, *de dilectis gravioribus*)

Other *latae sententiae* censures

1. Apostasy, heresy or schism: Apostasy, heresy or

schism: *latae sententiae* excommunication. (Canon 1364 § 1)

2. Physical force against a bishop: *latae sententiae* interdict and, if a cleric, *latae sententiae* suspension. (Canon 1370, § 2)

3. One who, apart from the case of a partner in a sin against the sixth commandment, though unable to give valid sacramental absolution, attempts to do so, or hears a sacramental confession: *latae sententiae* interdict and, if a cleric, *latae sententiae* suspension. (Canon 1378, § 2 2o)

4. False denunciation of a confessor of soliciting a penitent to commit a sin against the sixth commandment: *latae sententiae* interdict and, if a cleric, *latae sententiae* suspension. (Canon 1390, § 1)

5. A cleric who attempts marriage, even if only civilly: *latae sententiae* suspension. (Canon 1394 § 1)

6. A religious in perpetual vows who is not a cleric but who attempts marriage, even if only civilly: *latae sententiae* interdict. (Canon 1394, § 2)

7. A person who actually procures an abortion: *latae sententiae* excommunication. (Canon 1398)

Those who can incur penalties

Although a crime may carry with it a penalty, there are subjective circumstances that can prevent the penalty being incurred, such as lack of use of reason, ignorance of the law, under the age of 16 etc., and all these are dealt with in Canons 1321-1330.

Remission of *latae sententiae* in the internal forum (Canon 1357)

The cessation of penalties is covered in Canons 1354-1363. Canon 1357 deals specifically with the remission of *latae sententiae* censures in the internal sacramental forum which have not been declared.

Formula for Absolution from Censures

In the course of sacramental confession, it is not necessary to use any special formula for absolution from censures. It is enough that the confessor intend to absolve the penitent from the reserved sin. However, before absolving from sins, he may use the following formula of absolution from a censure outside the sacrament of penance: 'By the power granted to me I absolve you from the bond of excommunication (or suspension or interdict) in the name of the Father, and of the Son, and of the Holy Spirit.'

Postscript

In a recent book entitled *Friar Beyond the Pale* by Fr Wilfred McGreal, O.Carm., which is a biography of the late Fr. Elias Lynch, O. Carm., there is a letter from Fr Elias headed "Being sensitive when hearing confessions." In it he tells the story of how he went to confession in Dublin deliberately trying to avoid a priest whom, simply by his face, he judged to be proud and insensitive. As luck – or Providence – would have it, he found himself in this very man's confessional. Having a big problem on his mind, Fr Elias was especially looking for sympathy and now not expecting to find it. In fact, he came out of that confessional a changed man: "he received me with such understanding and sympathy that he resolved the whole matter for me. I was his last penitent that night, that Saturday night of all Saturday nights that changed my life." Fr Elias goes to say that whenever, as a confessor, we go into the confessional we should never be in a hurry and never say to ourselves: "This is just another one". We never know what the Holy Spirit may do through us each time we hear those words: "Bless me Father, for I have sinned. It's...weeks since my last confession..."

(Quoted by kind permission of the author.)

Acknowledgements

In the preparation of this small manual, I owe much to the unpublished lecture notes of the late Canon A.H. Couratin, M.A. For much of the material used in Chapter XII, I have used an unpublished lecture of the late Revd. D.L. Powell, M.A. Fr. Nicholas Halligan's *Sacraments of Reconciliation* Volume II (Alba House, New York), has also been of great assistance. Other acknowledgements have been included in the main body of the text. I should like to thank two of my colleagues, Fr John Boyle, B.Sc., M.Sc., J.C.L. and Fr Gerard Bradley, B.Mus., B.Th., A.K.C. for kindly reading the script and making some very useful suggestions, as well as correcting typing and other errors. Thanks also are due to students and staff of St John's Seminary, Wonersh who have patiently dealt with my computer illiteracy and subsequent problems. Not least, this manual could not have been written without experience gained from pastoral ministry in a number of parishes over many years and to those parishes I owe a great debt.